The Show and Tell Day

by Sibel Sagner
illustrated by Moni Perez

It was Show and Tell Day at school.
The children were happy.
They had things to show.
Everyone liked Show and Tell Day.

Show and Tell Day

‘I will go first,’ said Miss Garcia.

‘I will tell you about my family.
I have a mum, a dad
and two sisters.’

‘I like to take photos of my family.’

Miss Garcia showed her photographs
to the children.

'Here I am, on holiday
with my family,' she said.

‘Now it’s your turn, Omar,’
said Miss Garcia.

‘Come and show us your things.’

1 2 3 4 5
6 7 8 9 10

‘I like finding rocks and shells,’
said Omar.

‘I go down to the beach to find them.’

The children looked at the rocks
and shells.

Zara was next.

'I like to make animals from paper,' said Zara.

'I keep them in this box.'

‘I can make ladybirds and frogs and fish,’ said Zara.

‘I like this rabbit,’ said Leila.

Zara smiled. ‘I can show you how to make it,’ she said.

Beno came to show his kites
to the class.

'Look at this kite,' said Beno.
'It can fly very fast.'

‘Wow! Your kites are great,’ said Kofi.

‘Thanks,’ said Beno. ‘You can come and fly kites with me.’

'Well done, everyone,' said Miss Garcia.

'Now we will make a display on my big table.'

‘Oh no! We have too many things to show,’ said Omar.

‘We need a bigger table.’

The Show and Tell Day • Sibel Sagner

Teaching notes written by Sue Bodman and Glen Franklin

Using this book

Developing reading comprehension

This is a further book in the International School strand of Cambridge Reading Adventures. In this story, Miss Garcia holds a Show and Tell day, and the children share things about their home lives with their friends. Children have opportunity to apply their growing phonic knowledge to read new, unfamiliar words, as well as reading known high-frequency words automatically and fluently to support comprehension.

Grammar and sentence structure

- Sentences are growing in complexity, including the use of fronted adverbial phrases (*'Here I am'* on p.5) and more complex constructions (such as embedding the reporting clause in speech on p.13).
- Speech punctuation is used to indicate different characters speaking (see, for example, p.11).

Word meaning and spelling

- Opportunity to rehearse automatic fast recognition of high-frequency or regular words.
- Reading two-syllable words by identifying the known parts of words (*'everyone', 'display'*).

Curriculum links

Speaking and Listening – Host a Show and Tell Day and ask children to talk about their object and why they have chosen it.

Literacy – Children can display their Show and Tell items and write captions to accompany them. Use non-fiction texts to follow the conventions for how captions are written.

Learning Outcomes

Children can:

- solve unfamiliar words using print information and understanding of the text
- attend to the use of sentence structure and punctuation to support comprehension
- link their own experience to those of characters portrayed, explaining their reasons.

A guided reading lesson

Book Introduction

Give each child a copy of the book. Read the title and the blurb with them. Remind the children that they have read other books about Omar and his friends. (There is another International School story *A Day at the Museum* at Blue Band. Children may have already read this.)

Orientation

Ask: *What do you think the children and Miss Garcia are going to do in this story?* Establish what the children understand by a Show and Tell day, linking to prior knowledge of what happens in their own school setting.

Remind the children of (or establish) the characters in the story. Give a brief overview of the book:

In this book, Miss Garcia holds a Show and Tell day in school. The children can bring in anything they like to show the class. I wonder what they will bring ... Elicit some ideas from the children based on their prior reading and knowledge of characters, for example, that Omar likes to help.

Preparation

Pages 2 and 3: *Look at the children's boxes. What do you think Omar has in his box?* Draw attention to the phrase 'Show and